'AS YOU ARE
WELL AWARE, WE
NEVER LOVED
EACH OTHER IN
YOUR LIFETIME.
BOTH OF US
PRETENDED.'

GEORGES SIMENON

Born 1903, Liège, Belgium
Died 1989, Lausanne, Switzerland

First published in French as *Lettre à ma mère* in 1974.

SIMENON IN PENGUIN MODERN CLASSICS

GEORGES SIMENON

Letter to My Mother

Translated by Ralph Manheim

PENGUIN BOOKS

PENGUIN CLASSICS

UK | USA | Canada | Ireland | Australia
India | New Zealand | South Africa

Penguin Books is part of the Penguin Random House group
of companies whose addresses can be found at
global.penguinrandomhouse.com.

Penguin
Random House
UK

This edition first published 2018
001

Set in 10.2/12.75 pt Dante MT Std
Typeset by Jouve (UK), Milton Keynes
Printed in Great Britain by Clays Ltd, St Ives plc

ISBN: 978–0–241–33966–4

www.greenpenguin.co.uk

MIX
Paper from
responsible sources
FSC® C018179

Penguin Random House is committed to a
sustainable future for our business, our readers
and our planet. This book is made from Forest
Stewardship Council® certified paper.

Dear Mama,

It has been close to three and a half years since you died, at the age of ninety-one, and perhaps it's only now that I'm beginning to understand you. Throughout my childhood and adolescence I lived under one roof with you, I lived with you, but when I left for Paris at the age of nineteen, you were still a stranger to me.

Come to think of it, I never called you Mama, I called you Mother, just as I never called my father Papa. How did that come about? I don't know.

I went back to Liège now and then for short visits. The longest was the last, when I spent a whole week, day after day, at the Hôpital de Bavière – where as a boy I served at Mass – looking on at your death agony.

That expression, to be sure, hardly applies to the days that preceded your death. You lay in your bed, surrounded by relatives or persons unknown to me. There were some days when it was all I could do to get near you. I watched you for hours. You were not in pain. You had no fear of dying. And you didn't tell your beads from morning till night, though there was always a black-clad nun sitting there day after day in the same chair, in the same place.

Sometimes you smiled; often, in fact. But when I speak of you, the word 'smile' takes on a rather special meaning. You looked at us, at these people who would survive you and follow you to the graveyard, and now and then a widening of your lips gave you an ironic expression.

It seemed as though you were already in another world, or rather, in a world of your own, your familiar, inner world.

Even as a child, you see, I had known that smile. There was melancholy in it, and resignation. You endured life. You didn't live it.

You seemed to be waiting for the day when at last you would be lying in your hospital bed, resting, before going to your eternal rest.

Your doctor, who had performed the operation, was a childhood friend of mine. He told me you would die slowly and peacefully.

It took about a week, my longest stay in Liège since I had left it as a boy of nineteen. After visiting hours I couldn't resist the temptation to renew such pleasures of my youth as mussels with French fries and eel au vert.

Is it shameful to mingle gastronomic recollections with my memories of your hospital room?

I don't think so. They go together. Everything goes together to form the whole, which I am trying now to unravel and which, to judge by the way you looked at me, with an expression of mingled indifference and tenderness, you may have understood before I did.

As you are well aware, we never loved each other in your lifetime. Both of us pretended.

Today I believe that the images we had of each other were both false.

Can it be that the knowledge that one is dying makes one more lucid than ever before? I don't know yet. But I am just about certain that you classified the people who came to see you, the nephews, nieces, neighbours, and so on, very accurately.

And the moment I arrived, you classified me as well.

But it wasn't your image of me that I looked for in your eyes and calm features: what I was beginning to see was a true image of you.

*

I was anxious and unnerved. The day before, I had received a phone call from Orban, my old schoolmate, now head surgeon at the Hôpital de Bavière, who had operated on you, I had driven with all possible speed over Swiss roads, the German Autobahn, and a bit of Belgian highway.

I suddenly found myself facing the big varnished door of the Hôpital de Bavière, where as a child I used to pull up panting, especially in the winter, after a breathless run through the deserted neighbourhood, keeping to the middle of the street because I was afraid.

I found your pavilion right away. And then your door. I knocked and someone called out: 'Come in.'

It gave me a shock to see at least four or five people in your little hospital room, not to mention a nun all in black, who seemed to be on guard, like a sentry.

I made my way through to your bed to kiss you. And then you said very simply, as if it were the most natural thing in the world to say:

'Why have you come, Georges?'

That little sentence weighed on my mind, and I thought about it later on. Maybe it has told me something about you.

I kissed you on the forehead. Someone, I don't remember who, stood up and gave me his chair. I looked at you intensely. I think I had never in all my life looked at you in that way.

I had expected to find you moribund, in a semi-coma. I rediscovered your eyes, which I have tried to describe but which I shall have to describe again, because it was some time before I began to understand them.

Were you surprised to see me? Did you suppose I wouldn't come to be with you in your death agony and attend your funeral? Did you think I was indifferent, or even hostile?

Was the look in those pale-grey eyes one of genuine surprise, or was that one of your tricks? I can't help thinking that you knew I'd come and were expecting me, but that since you had always distrusted everyone and me in particular, you were afraid I would not come.

The people around you didn't have the tact to leave the room. I had to put them out by telling them I wanted to be alone with my mother for a little while.

The nun didn't budge. She stayed there in her chair, as motionless, as impenetrable, and, I'm certain, as indifferent as a statue. She never said a word of greeting when I came in. She never said goodbye when I left.

It looked as if she had the keys to the gates of death, heaven and hell, and was waiting for the right time to make use of them.

For a long while you and I just looked at each other. There was no sadness in your face. There was no emotion I could identify for sure.

Triumph? Possibly. You were the thirteenth of thirteen children. Your father was ruined before you were born. You were five years old when he died.

That was your start in life. You were left alone with your mother. Your brothers and sisters had all gone off, some to the graveyard. You lived in a modest, extremely modest, apartment, in a poor neighbour-hood in Liège, and I've never known what you and your mother lived on until you were nineteen and went to work as a salesgirl in a depart-ment store.

I have a bad photograph of you, dating from that time. You were pretty; your face still had the roundness of youth, but in your eyes I see an iron will and distrust, distrust of the whole world.

There was a shadow of a smile on your lips, but there was nothing youthful about that smile; it was full of bitterness, and your eyes, fixed on the camera lens, were hard.

'Why have you come, Georges?'

Perhaps those few words are the key to your whole life.

When we were left alone, except for the nun, you couldn't think of anything to say to me, nor I to you. Your emaciated hand was resting on the bed sheet, and I took it. There was no warmth in your hand; it seemed lifeless.

Would you really have been disappointed or grieved if I hadn't come? I wonder.

You knew those people who were cluttering up your room when I arrived; you knew, in a manner of speaking, what each one of them expected of you. Money, one of your two dining-room cupboards, linen, and so on.

Because you've never had illusions. You've never trusted anyone. As far back as I can remember, you've suspected everyone of falsehood, of ulterior motives.

I wasn't six yet, I'd just started school at the Institut Saint-André, when you first thought I was telling you lies. You've thought so ever since. The last time you came to see me was at Epalinges. I'd invited you to spend a few weeks with me. You were already very old and infirm, and I was secretly thinking of sending you to one of the excellent rest homes in the region.

Epalinges, which I put up for sale two years ago and haven't sold yet, is an enormous, rather luxurious house. It required a large staff. You spent the better part of your days in the garden, in the dancing shadow of a birch tree.

Your main worry was not how you would spend the last years of your life. When you managed to corner a member of the staff, and an anxious look came into your eyes and you asked: 'Has this property really been paid for?'

You'd had the same worry when I invited you to La Richardière. La Richardière was an estate with a big pond full of ducks, an enormous vegetable garden, a forest and a few meadows. There too you spent a good part of your time out of doors in an easy chair. I seem to remember that I had three horses at the time. They required a groom. A gardener took care of the garden and barnyard. There too, in short, I had considerable help. That was in 1931.

You observed their comings and goings. You kept your eye on them. And once when you were alone with Boule, you asked: 'Has my son a lot of debts?'

In fifty years I've never been able to convince you that I work and make a living.

Your distrust wasn't confined to me. It was innate in you. The fatherless five-year-old, left alone with her mother, couldn't believe in miracles.

But, at bottom, I was the main object of your distrust.

Was it love? Fear that I'd get into trouble? Were you afraid that I was mixed up in some shady business?

No one but you knows the answer, Mother. I can only conjecture, and there perhaps the days I spent at your beside have helped me.

I have just called you Mother rather than Mama. You see, I've been accustomed to calling you Mother since my earliest childhood. I have a good many childhood memories, more than most people. My memory of recent events is often sketchy, but I remember the first years of my life very clearly.

I wonder if you ever took me on your lap. If you did, it left no trace in my memory, which means that it didn't happen very often.

I don't believe that the 'Father' and 'Mother' I was taught to use originated with you, and I can't hold it against you. My father was a soft-hearted man, but, like all the Simenons I've known, he was not expansive.

I remember a trifling incident that may be significant. One day, in a moment of discouragement, you said to him: 'When I think, Désiré, that I've never heard you say: "I love you."'

My father answered – with tears in his eyes, I'm sure: 'But you're here.'

Is that what hardened you? Can it be that you felt torn between your own family, the Brülls, and the Simenon tribe you married into, and that this feeling threw you off balance?

I shall try to understand all that, Mother, and tell you about it.

*

I spent nineteen years of my life with you and about the same with Désiré. You worked very hard. So did he. Fate didn't grant you much joy.

Today I realize that a couple with children is not just a couple. And sometimes they forget it. Near them in the house, almost always present, there are children who watch them and, in the measure of their intelligence, judge them.

The parents think of themselves as simply a father and a mother.

But they are wrong. They are two individuals, whose every gesture, word, and glance are judged mercilessly.

Now that you're dead, now that I'm writing you one of my rare letters, I too am a father. It goes without saying that I've ceased to be merciless.

Today I wonder what you, always so distrustful, were thinking in the hours I spent at the foot of your bed, looking at you more intensely than I might have wished. Maybe you said to yourself: 'He's impatient for me to pass on so he can leave the hospital and go back home.'

And maybe the shadow of a smile that crossed your lips every morning meant: 'Look! I'm still here . . .'

Actually, I was trying all that time to understand you, to imagine the little Henriette Brüll you once were, for you never really know a person unless you've known his childhood.

My knowledge of yours is fragmentary, and quite possibly there's as much legend as reality in what I do know. You spoke of your childhood as little as possible, and in those days children didn't dare question their parents about their past.

I know the rue Féronstrée and all the little side streets. I know that you lived with your mother on one of those side streets. I also know *that you didn't speak French, but only a kind of Flemish mixed with German, which made people laugh at you in the shops when you were sent out to buy this or that.*

To me, your father is also a legendary figure. He was the manager of a large estate in Limbourg, bordering on the canal. Some cousins look after it now, and I used to spend vacations there. Your father was dyjk-master (master of the dykes), and you were rightly proud of his position. The dyjkmaster keeps the keys to the sluices that are used to flood the region in time of drought, and that makes him an important person.

Why did he leave Limbourg? You never told me. Next I remember him at Herstal, in the suburbs of Liège, living with his family in the old château that once belonged to Pepin of Herstal. He owned four or five barges and, I believe, had a big lumber business.

I have a photograph of him. He was a man with a strong face and hard eyes. A German, born near the Dutch border, and the girl he married was Dutch.

How and why did he move to Belgium? Why, when he was about fifty, did he start drinking to excess? I don't know. But I do know that one night when he was drunk he countersigned some promissory notes for a friend and was ruined when that friend went bankrupt.

You were five years old when you left the old château in Herstal. The only memory of the château you ever confided to me was that you had a ewe. She had been given to you when she was still a lamb, and when she grew up you refused to part with her.

What kind of life did you lead in Herstal? Under what circumstances did your brothers and sisters, who were all much older than you, drift away?

You see, I'd have liked to know all that, because it would have helped me to know the mother you became.

There are big gaps in your story as it was told to me. I have a photograph of your mother, a haughty woman; her features are regular but as hard as her husband's, and her eyes look straight ahead, as though defying the world.

That was the woman who, when someone knocked at the door of the apartment, quickly put pots on the stove to make people think she was preparing a lavish meal.

You took after her in a way. But there was also a big difference. You too were proud, Mother, but, if you see what I mean, you had the pride of your humility. You were proud to be poor and never ask for anything. You pretended to be poorer than you were, as if it were a virtue, and now, at the age of seventy-one, I'm beginning to think it might be.

I often heard you say these words: 'You see, Maria, we manage with the strict minimum.'

Those words – 'the strict minimum' – haunted me as a child. I regarded them as an insult to my father, because in marrying you and founding a family, he had shown that he was capable of living up to his responsibilities.

But you were a Brüll, and the Brülls have never resigned themselves to modest circumstances, let alone poverty.

One of your brothers, whom I've seen only once in my life, was rich. He owned a château. Like your father, he was an important man in Limbourg, where he sold fertilizer and seed to the farmers and bought their produce.

That brother never went to see you after your marriage. He never set foot in our house. But one day when I was looking at a piece of furniture made of white pine painted to look like oak, you confided to me: 'My mother and I kept a few pieces of old furniture from my father's day. One day my brother came to the house. He said that rickety old furniture was no good and he'd get us some new things instead.'

My uncle had our family antiques carted away and generously replaced them with stuff from a cheap furniture store.

You understood. Now I know that you understood a good many things and that little by little an accumulation of experiences unknown to me made you into the woman who became my mother.

I watched you. I observed the expression of your eyes when this one and that one came in. And now and then I saw you lower your lids, as though you were sick of the whole business, of these visitors and of me as well.

*

Your father died when you were only five. You hardly knew him. Did you know your mother much longer? I don't know when she died or what she died of. Nor do I know how old you were or what effect her death may have had on you and your life.

The discovery that two generations can be so far apart leaves me aghast, for all of us, by virtue of our genes if not of our upbringing, resemble our parents in some measure.

Knowing you as I do, you must have been wondering, as you lay motionless in your hospital bed, what I was thinking about in the hours I spent looking at you. As I've already told you, I have only one photograph of your father, and to me he remains an extraordinary and mysterious figure.

I searched your face for features resembling his. In the end I found one: your thin, almost always closed lips, which even in smiling did not part, but only widened a little.

Did you take after your father? In any case, I discovered no point of resemblance to your mother, whose picture I also have in our family album. On the contrary. As far as I can judge, your mother's reaction to her sudden poverty was to hold her head high and to look at the world with haughty, serene contempt.

You tended, however, to bow your head. You humbled yourself. You said 'thank you'. You said 'thank you' to everyone and everything, to the woman who sold you milk and even to your sisters.

But wasn't that 'thank you', which you taught me, an expression of inward pride?

I'd have liked to know everything that happened when my grandfather was ruined. That château in Herstal had been torn down by the time I was old enough to look around me. I didn't see my uncles and aunts until they were old.

You were the last child, born at a time when no more children were expected; you might have been the daughter of one of your brothers or sisters. In fact, you were the same age as some of my cousins.

In the last years of his life, your father, as I know because it was part of the family legend, drank a good deal and was drunk more often than not.

As I've already told you, the legend has him signing notes for a local notable who frequented the cafés with him. The notable went bankrupt and your father was obliged to honour the notes he had countersigned.

I know the man's name. I used to see it in big white letters on big wagons drawn by two horses, which went about the city when I was little.

Later on, there was an incident that I was careful not to mention to you. In 1952, I went to Belgium to attend a reception at the Belgian Academy. Of course I stopped at Liège. You were still living in one of those plain little houses in the Place du Congrès quarter, where I spent my childhood.

Liège had arranged an unexpected welcome for me, consisting of official receptions and no less official luncheons and dinners. You attended them with me.

But one evening, some journalists took me to a dinner that was not part of the programme, near Embourg, where we spent so many of our vacations.

I found myself in a large, comfortable, not to say luxurious, villa. A sumptuous dinner had been prepared for me.

I had been smoking a pipe with a gold band, a present the Liège journalists had given me that same day. I put it down beside my plate.

After dinner the lady of the house came over to me, bubbling with excitement. She was still young and rather good-looking in a well-fed way.

'Did you realize, Monsieur Simenon, that your family and mine have been acquainted for many years?'

What could I say? I realized nothing. What with all the dinners and receptions I was being dragged to, I didn't even know my hostess's name.

'I am the daughter of Monsieur X . . . He was a friend of your grandfather . . .'

I stiffened and came very close to leaving the house without a word. She was the daughter of the man for whom my grandfather had ruined himself.

I stayed a few minutes more and then I left, thinking of the little five-year-old girl you had been. The next day I noticed that I didn't have the 'commemorative' pipe my Liège colleagues had given me. I mentioned it to one of them, who proceeded to investigate.

The pipe was found. My hostess's son had taken it and hidden it in his room.

So you see, we were robbed twice by the same family.

The pipe didn't matter. What did matter was the time, so important in my life, between the year you were five and the day when, bashful, plump and seventeen, you applied for work at the Innovation Department Store.

Did your father survive his ruin for long? I don't know. All I know is that he died of cancer. How old were your brothers? And your sisters? What were your relations with them?

I can't help thinking of you at that time as a little bird fallen from the nest.

The whole family, from what I can make out, sometimes spoke German, your father's language, and sometimes Flemish, the language of your Dutch mother.

I can see you in the shops of the rue Féronstrée, a bustling business street like the rue Puits-en-Stock where my father was born, stammering the few words of French you had picked up here and there.

Where did you go to school? Wherever it was, you were a little foreigner, and the others must have made fun of you. Every word of French had to be explained. And when you went back to your mother's little apartment, you fell back into the mixture of German and Flemish that I heard you talking all your life with your brothers and sisters.

It came naturally to you and your family. My father could only sit quietly in his corner, excluded from your family secrets.

During your last days, as you lay peacefully with a thin smile on your fine lips, did you sometimes think of the sheep you had as a little girl, of your father's horse-drawn canal barges, of the tree trunks they carried, and the piles of wood around the château in Herstal?

You hardly ever spoke to us of those things, and I had the impression that in your hospital bed you reviewed images that no longer belonged to anyone but you.

Your brothers and sisters were dead, for they were much older than you, and you were ninety-one. The little last-born had held up staunchly to the very end. What seems even more extraordinary is that in the last years, after all your brothers' and sisters' families had drifted apart as families do, it was with you that your brothers and sisters sought refuge.

The others all came from the other side of the river. The Outremeuse quarter in Liège is reputed to be lower middle class, if not actually poor.

And yet one after another they rented houses there in order to be nearer to you.

I won't go so far as to speak of poetic justice. But I'm sure the thought crossed your mind, for when as a young girl you suddenly lost weight, when your nerves were so frayed that you'd burst into tears for no reason at all, those same brothers and sisters used to say you looked like the cat's canary.

The cat's canary buried them all.

*

I wonder, as I write to you, if sometimes, in the course of the hours we spent looking, almost staring, at each other in silence, we both thought of the same things. One memory that came back to me was a distressing one. It had to do with an incident that I'm ashamed of – and there haven't been many events in my life that I have reason to be ashamed of.

It happened during my visit to Liège in 1952. D., my second wife, was with me. She tried to make herself as important as possible.

The mayor and the municipal authorities had arranged a magnificent welcome for me. Among other things, they had organized a luncheon at the Ansembourg Museum, an old patrician mansion that had been preserved in its original state, with all its furniture, paintings, carpets and knickknacks.

A chamber orchestra, placed in an alcove off the monumental dining room, played César Franck, Grétry and Mozart.

But the incident occurred before they began to play. You saw a small place card with your name on it to the right of the place that had been reserved for me. D. snatched it up and said in a peremptory tone: 'Over here, Mama.'

And she led you to the place that was supposed to be hers.

Did anyone notice? I believe so. As for me, I didn't have the gumption to intervene, but I was so ashamed of myself that during the meal

I paid no attention to the music, nor to the speeches afterward.

It's one of my most unpleasant memories.

To cancel it out, so to speak, with a more amusing memory dating from the same visit, let me remind you of a dinner at one of the city's big beer halls. My journalist colleagues, some of whom I had worked with in the old days, had let the officials take up the greater part of my time. All they asked for was one evening, an informal dinner at this beer hall.

But they suggested that I'd better not take you with me, because the free-and-easy get-together they had in mind might end in a kind of gaiety that wouldn't be to your liking.

So I told you you weren't invited that evening.

You always took the darkest view of anything connected with me. Sometimes you knew best. But more often you were mistaken.

I can still see you shaking your head in disapproval and hear you saying: 'Good heavens, Georges, be careful what you do. You'll see, they're going to drag you into an orgy.'

Of course there was no orgy.

I never understood your deep-seated, almost innate distrust of me. You had it as far back as I can remember, beginning in my earliest childhood, and it was probably one of the reasons for the barrier between us. You always seemed to suspect me of the worst misdeeds. Once, for instance, when my brother Christian, who was three years younger than I, began to cry, you turned to me and asked: 'Now what have you done to him?'

I hadn't done anything to him. He was crying for some reason that had nothing to do with me. It seems to me now that perhaps you needed a villain in the family, and that villain was me.

I don't hold it against you. But I've had my resentful moments – in the early forties, for instance, when I put you into Pedigree under the name of Elise. I realize now that the rather elaborate portrait I drew of you was not accurate.

As a matter of fact, I avoided publishing it at the time. I kept it in a drawer for more than ten years, for fear of distressing you. When the book finally did appear, I was surprised to hear through neighbours that you were proud of it, that you made everyone you met read it and signed your letters Elise instead of Henriette.

What pleased me most was to learn that after my visit to Liège, the one I've just been telling you about, the authorities, from the mayor to the governor, not only invited you to all their official dinners and ceremonies, but also sent a car to pick you up.

You see, I have good and bad memories, like everyone else, I suppose, and I imagine that in your room at the Hôpital de Bavière it occurred to you too now and then that maybe I wasn't as 'bad' as you had imagined.

A little later I invited you to come and stay with me in Connecticut for as long as you pleased. I had a big place there, and I was rather afraid you'd react as you always did when you detected anything approaching luxury in my life and surroundings.

I picked you up in my car at the international airport. To my consternation, you were dressed like a beggarwoman, though I knew for a fact that a relative of ours, who owned a number of dress shops, had provided you with an ample wardrobe.

When we got home, I asked you if you had anything else to put on and you said no. Out of defiance, so to speak. Yes, defiance, but a defiance that I now understand and am tempted to approve.

Instinctively, the little last-born of the rue Féronstrée, the salesgirl at the Innovation, whom her brothers, wealthy as they were by then, had never helped, rebelled against anything that was expensive.

'Ah, Maria, to think that I manage on the strict minimum . . .'

It all fits in. I took you to New York and bought you several dresses. And this is the place for a little tragicomic story, more tragic than comic in the end.

D. always made it her business to root through other people's drawers and belongings. She discovered that you had only one old corset, which was all frayed and out of shape. She went out and bought you another, and without mentioning it to you, threw the old one in the garbage pail.

Next morning she was amazed to find that the corset was gone. You must have got up during the night, made your way through the rather complicated corridors, opened the door God knows how, and scurried along the walls like a mouse until you found the garbage pails. You never said a word. Nobody said a word. That same night, D., who was really stubborn, put the corset back in the garbage. And once again you went and took it out.

It got to be a battle between two women, between two wills. On the one side D., haughty, aggressive, merciless, and on the other the little woman who had come from Liège wearing the oldest clothes she had, as though to proclaim: 'You invited me. You insisted on my coming. Well, you'll have to take me as I am, because you can't impress me with your fancy ways.'

Has that ever come up in your thoughts, Mother? It has in mine, and I've thought of a good many other things that I'll try to tell you about, things that have been tucked away at the bottom of my mind for years.

Face to face in a little hospital room with someone who has only a few days to live, a man tends to search his mind, and to do it honestly, without evasions.

*

These people coming and going in your room don't concern me. They don't even seem to be coming and going. Their steps are so muffled I don't even hear them arriving or leaving. Seated, if they find a chair, or standing, there they stay, apparently for hours on end, no doubt waiting to see death come.

The only unchanging fixture is the nun. There she sits in waxen immobility, holding a rosary of enormous brown beads in her lap. What she's waiting for, I have no idea. Probably the same thing as the others.

The most faithful visitor is a rather portly gentleman, some sort of distant relative, who's written to me two or three times, asking me to buy a house in the vicinity of Liège for him and his family. I haven't told you about him. But I know that you've guessed.

For all intents and purposes, we're alone, confronting each other, as it were. You're ninety-one, but in my eyes you haven't aged. You've always had that thin face, that lustreless complexion, those lips that widen now and then.

As for me, I'm about seventy. Between us there's a gulf of fifty years. I know next to nothing about your life during those years – and still less about the years that preceded them.

How is it that you, the youngest in the family, should be in possession of the family album? Your elder brothers and sisters must have laid claim to it. Did you get it by sheer obstinacy, like everything else you've got in your life?

It's a big album bound in green leather, with gilt corners and a gilt flower on the cover.

I've often questioned you about the people in it. People didn't have cameras in those days. You had to go to the photographer's, and he'd hide his face behind a black cloth while he brought you into focus. You didn't do it very often, only on great occasions.

Your father and mother figure prominently. I also recognize some of your sisters and brothers-in-law, whom I met when I was little.

But there were others you could never tell me anything about. I wonder if you yourself knew who they were. I am thinking in particular of a woman with a rigid posture, an austere face, and a set gaze, wearing a uniform I've never seen, that of some German religious sect, I believe someone told me. And a young man in the uniform of an officer in the Kaiser's army, who must have been one of my uncles.

But now, as I look at you, it's not of them that I'm thinking, but of another photograph: a very young woman, who hasn't quite finished growing, with a black crêpe veil hanging down to the ground from her little hat, which is also of black crêpe.

It's you. At what age, I don't know. I don't know whom you were in mourning for. Do you yourself know? There were so many deaths in the family at that time that I saw you and your sisters more often in crêpe veils than in coloured dresses.

Sometimes I wonder if we, you in your bed and I in an uncomfortable chair, haven't been playing a strange little game all these days.

You know you're going to die. My friend Orban didn't try to hide it from you, and he was right. It's never been easy to hide anything from you.

So in a manner of speaking you're already living outside the world, the world of living creatures, that is, and you look at us with a certain irony, but also with pity.

Because we, who are looking at you too, still have a road to travel. And no one can tell us how long that road will be or what it will be like.

Whereas you know, and in that you're superior to us. Maybe that accounts for the smile that crosses your lips from time to time.

But then you were young, seventeen. That's the age I give the young woman in mourning in the photograph. Maybe eighteen. Your features still had a certain childlike haze about them.

It was about that time that you applied for work at the Innovation, one of the Liège department stores. Full of self-confidence, as you've often told me, with an almost defiant look in your eyes, you went to see a certain Monsieur Bernheim, who was then manager of the store.

You see, I've even remembered his name. Monsieur Bernheim. That name stands for a phase in your life, because the very next day you went to work behind a counter.

I often went to the Innovation with you when I was little. You knew most of the salesgirls. You went from counter to counter shaking hands and exchanging news.

Your news couldn't have been very cheerful, because at the end of those exchanges you were usually holding a handkerchief to your eyes.

I'd have liked, and I'd still like, to have a photograph of you when you were really a child, when your father had just died and you went to live near the rue Féronstrée with your mother. There's none in the album. A big chunk of your past that has left no trace, and those are the very years that interest me the most.

I have every reason to suppose that even as a little girl you were *highly strung and hypersensitive, but that by some miracle you managed to keep your balance and will power.*

Will power is something you've had all your life, and now that you're lying here in your hospital bed that will be your deathbed, I'm not sure you didn't choose the time of your death. I wouldn't put it past you!

Another mystery: how did you and my father meet? In the department where you worked at the Innovation you had a friend, Valérie, who was as small as you but very homely. You were very close. When you saw Désiré passing outside the plate-glass window, one of you, I don't know whether it was you or Valérie, would say: 'What a lovely walk!'

Because my father, who was slender and over six feet tall, walked in long strides, with the regularity of a metronome.

Was it through that window that you first made contact and that what represented love in your life was born? When I was a child, and later, when I began to be a man, no one ever spoke of such things in the family.

Every day at the same time, Désiré kissed his mother goodbye on the rue Puits-en-Stock and started mechanically for his office, which was near the Guillemins station. He was already one of the top clerks at the insurance company where he worked, for he was the only one with a high-school education.

On his way home for lunch, did Désiré go almost half an hour out of his way to peer at you through the Innovation window?

Had he noticed you before? Had he fallen in love with the tiny girl with the hair so blonde it was almost white?

Again, I don't know. It's taken me till the age of seventy and then *some to realize that not only my whole past, but also yours and my father's, which played so important a part in moulding my personality, are a blank wall to me.*

An occasional silhouette, a few familiar and more unfamiliar faces in the photograph album. Snatches of sentences caught here and there.

At least two of your sisters were as highly strung as you, highly strung and impressionable, which doesn't mean unbalanced, though one of them died in what was then called an insane asylum, and another drank herself to death in her forties.

In any case, you were abnormally sensitive, and I'm not the only one to have inherited that condition from you. As a child and young man, I often walked in my sleep. Several times you caught me at the street corner in my flannel nightshirt. The doctor advised you to put bars on my windows, and until I left Liège I had those bars before my eyes, rather like a prisoner.

I still have spells of sleepwalking, which is very unusual at my age. Two of my sons walk in their sleep, though they were not born of the same mother. And my grandson does it too.

Does it come from you? Probably, because my father was a calm man; I never saw him in a nervous state, and he never lost his self-control.

It's the little girl from the rue Féronstrée that I take after, and that's why I'm scrutinizing you so intensely.

Was it a reaction to your unsettled nerves that made you look for security above all else?

At that time there were neither old-age pensions nor social security. A protracted illness could wreck a family.

Poor Désiré had a job that offered no pension, no guarantees of security.

'When I think that you never even took out life insurance!'

I often heard those words when you were in a bad mood. Désiré averted his eyes and said nothing; there was nothing for him to say.

His doctor told me why later on, after he had died of angina pectoris at the age of forty-four.

He had already had a heart condition when he was twenty-five. The insurance companies, including the one he worked for, had put him down as what is known rather inelegantly as 'a poor risk'.

He kept silent to the end. I don't hold it against you. It wasn't Désiré whom you held up to me as a model, but a certain Monsieur Reculé, a man in his sixties who had somehow – the ins and outs are unknown to me – became a kind of friend of the family.

He had stopped working; he had no need to work, because he was pensioned.

He had worked for the North Belgian Railways, and the railways had already introduced retirement pensions.

You could see him walking about, smiling, sure of himself, reaping the benefits of all the years he had spent at a ticket window. He didn't even have to worry about his wife's future, because when he died she too would receive a pension.

You see, Mother, that children watch and listen. Because of my father's illness, or rather because he had no insurance, you tried to shunt me into the civil service, to send me to a ticket window or office at the North Belgian Railways or some other company of the kind.

Can I hold it against you?

*

By curious meanders of thought I am filling in a blank in the story of your youth. I was wondering as I looked at you if the dying ever shed tears, and if you yourself would shed some.

It's the word 'tears' that touched off a memory.

You had a sister who was married to a wholesale grocer, the same sister, a fine-looking woman, who later drank herself to death. She had first a son, then a daughter.

Your mother must have been dead by then, for they took you in, not as a sister but as a nursemaid. You didn't eat at the table with them. You took your meals in the kitchen with two or three other servants. Not only did you take care of one child, then of both, but when you weren't busy with the children, they gave you other things to do.

If thinking of tears made me remember that, it's because I've heard you say that you never cried so much in all your life.

My uncle was a hard man. My aunt, your sister, was sometimes the most affectionate of women, and sometimes the most hateful.

I remember her well. The ground floor of the house was taken up with the store, which sold to small grocers and market women. When you went to see your sister, you knew instantly which mood she was in.

Either she'd insist on stuffing your shopping bag full of sardines and other canned goods, which you tried in vain to refuse, or she'd snarl at you: 'Look who's come begging again!'

I can imagine the life you led when you worked for them. You were the poor little maid of all work, who never dared to protest. I don't doubt for a moment that you cried a good deal.

How did you summon up the courage to walk out and go and live by yourself? Where did you spend your nights? Who gave you the idea of asking Monsieur Bernheim for a job?

You see that if we weren't living face to face in silence, I'd have a good many questions to ask you.

Maybe you lived with Valérie and her mother, whom I knew well. They were so tiny they might have been taken for two midgets, and they had strange monkeylike faces, but as you used to say, their hearts were in the right place.

Like all office workers in those days, Désiré wore a top hat. I've heard you speak of his lovely walk. I've also heard you speak of his 'lovely way of lifting his hat'.

Did he pluck up the courage one evening when the stores had closed to approach you and Valérie, lifting his hat in his lovely way? And if he did, what words did he stammer? For he was very bashful.

He belonged to a dramatic group at the church guild. But he never appeared on the stage. For years he preferred the prompter's box.

How could such a man have had the courage to accost you at a time when accosting a woman in the street was thought to be in very bad taste?

How long were you engaged?

He was very tall, over six feet, and you were tiny, about five foot two. It must have been very hard for the two of you to walk arm in arm.

You introduced him to your sister, whose children you had taken care of, and they advised you against marrying a common clerk with no future.

My father introduced you to his parents in the kitchen behind the hat shop on the rue Puits-en-Stock, and the whole Simenon tribe stiffened at the sight of the blushing little Flemish girl.

There had never been any Flemings in the family. And you weren't really Flemish. You were Flemish, or rather Dutch, only through your mother, whose parents owned a big farm in Dutch Limbourg.

They were proud people, they had property, but you hadn't inherited any of it. You hadn't inherited anything, except the little white-pine cupboard painted to look like oak, which I remember well and have already mentioned.

Where did you and Désiré go on Sundays? Not to the theatre. There weren't any movies. My father never set foot in a café, except for his game of cards on Sunday morning.

No doubt you went walking in the Avroy park, as I did later on with the two of you. I called it the duck park, because there was a pond full of ducks.

I have no pictures of your wedding or of that period of your life with Désiré. Knowing my father, I imagine he must have taken you on Sunday mornings to the kitchen on the rue Puits-en-Stock, where all the Simenons gathered around his father and mother.

Did they speak to you? Did you dare to open your mouth? I doubt it. The Simenons were such a closed corporation that you must have felt as far away as in a foreign country.

For a little more than a year you lived on the rue Léopold, in the centre of town, and it's there that I was born. Then you moved to the Outremeuse quarter, two steps from the rue Puits-en-Stock, and there you stayed.

You are now ninety-one. I shall soon be more than seventy. And all these years have come between us. Have they marked you? Do you still remember the days and hours?

To judge by your face, you seem rather relieved to see the end approaching.

I've spoken of the little mouse who scurried along the walls in

Lakeville to recover her corset. All your life you've scurried like a lit-tle mouse. I've seldom seen you seated. And now, maybe for the first time, I see you lying down.

I wonder, as I watch your face that has changed so little, your light-blue eyes that have kept their sparkle, whether your last sigh won't be a sigh of relief.

There is something in your hospital room that rather oppresses me and sometimes prevents me from thinking. It's the silence, broken only at long intervals by the scraping of a chair against the floor when someone leaves, the muffled steps of someone coming in, the embar-rassed mumblings with which the newcomers address you. It's very much like a church. Lying still at the centre of this church, you take on extraordinary dimensions.

For you dominate us all, all the strangers coming and going, among whom I should probably count myself, because to you I was a stranger. Now and then the door opens and closes silently, letting in a whiff of fresh air.

Only the padre's visit changes the atmosphere. He is tall and pow-erfully built, rather jovial in his daily life, I should think.

The moment he appears, everyone leaves, including me. Only the nun with the rosary remains in her chair.

Little groups form in the corridor. From time to time a patient is rolled past. Their eyes, as far as one can see, are blank or resigned.

Stubbornly, I keep looking for your truth; that is, I keep trying to understand you.

In *Pedigree*, you were a rather sketchy character. I recorded some of your words and deeds.

Today, I'm looking for the soul of the real Henriette.

On the rue Léopold, where you spent the first year of your married life, you and my father had a two-room apartment above a hat shop. When you needed water, you had to go down to the tap half a storey below.

It was an apartment for humble folk. I have the feeling that all your life you wanted to be identified with the humble folk.

You'd be very much surprised to hear that at my age I'm moving closer and closer to them, because I feel that their world is mine and that it's the only real world of truth.

In your eyes, Monsieur Reculé, with his railway pension, represented security. I also remember another man who, God knows how and why, became a friend of ours for a while.

His name was Monsieur Rorive. He was a short, pudgy man with a pink baby face. He was unusually careful about his appearance; I even suspect that he carried a rag in his pocket to wipe his yellow shoes with, in case a speck of dust should fall on them.

Monsieur Rorive had kept a dairy store; for many years he had lived amid the sweetish-sourish smell of butter and cheese. His wife was no taller than he and just as fat.

To see the two of them, neat, clean and well-dressed, with a guileless smile on their lips, one couldn't help feeling that life had been good to them.

You were full of admiration for Monsieur and Madame Rorive. One day you even asked your brother, the one who owned the château, to lend you a little money to open a dairy store. Your brother refused. He was a businessman; dairy stores and little sisters weren't in his line.

So, determined to make some money even if it killed you, to provide for your future and make sure you would never again suffer want, you persuaded Désiré to rent a small house not far from the one where we'd been living.

The houses in the neighbourhood were unimpressive, almost all alike except for the colour of the door and window frames. You hung out a modest sign: 'Furnished Rooms to Let.'

I wonder as I look at you, so frail in your bed, if it was cruelty on your part. You must have known my father's character. He was a man who liked his peace and quiet, his wicker chair, slippers and newspaper when he came home in the evening.

After only three years of marriage, little Henriette, whom her sisters called the cat's canary, imposed her will on big Désiré.

I held it against you. Child as I was, I had a feeling that the household was out of kilter, that no one mattered but you. You worked hard from morning to night, you wore your fingers to the bone doing huge piles of laundry, and often as not when your husband came home he found a Pole or a Russian reading his newspaper in his chair.

Now I know that it wasn't malice or even selfishness on your part. Like my uncle in his château, you followed your bent, and no sentiment could stop you.

When I was only eight or nine, they took one of your sisters away to an insane asylum. I was there, and I was terrified. I remember the cab at the door and the husband sobbing, with his hands braced against the wall and his head between his hands.

I said to myself, today I admit it: 'What if someday a cab came and took my mother away.'

They said you were a bundle of nerves. That meant you reacted intensely to the slightest setbacks, the slightest pinpricks.

I remember certain Sunday afternoons, for instance. In the morning we had decided to go walking in the country, but not far from Liège, because our only means of transportation was the streetcar. After lunch you were in your room putting up your bun. You were having trouble, it kept coming undone, you got more and more frantic, tears came to your eyes, and in the end you threw yourself on the bed sobbing.

My brother and I were ready, both in our Sunday best. Impatient, at a loss to understand, we waited on the pavement.

My father, who was also ready, kept shuttling from us to you and from you to us.

'Just another few minutes, children. Your mother isn't feeling well.'

It happened a hundred times, two hundred times. Christian and I didn't dare to show ourselves. Sometimes we heard screams, and then long, gasping, reproachful monologues.

The reproaches were addressed to my father, who was always calm and patient.

How were you able to put up with some of those roomers, who, rather than spend money heating their rooms, invaded the kitchen and almost crowded you out?

With them you were always smiling. I wondered why. Now I know: those roomers represented what I later heard you call your old age.

Désiré, with his modest but adequate monthly wage, wouldn't be there forever. You refused to count on us, your children.

Provision had to be made for your old age. There may have been a bit of madness in that obsession. Your sister had died insane. Your father had died young and in a rather odd way. He had found a *certain stability, or instability, in liquor, and it had led him to ruin his family. One of your brothers had ended up as a kind of tramp; we used to see him now and then, zigzagging aimlessly down the street.*

And when friends came to see my cousin, the wholesale grocer's daughter, she locked her mother in her room, for fear they'd see her drunk.

You never drank, except for a glass of light wine on New Year's Day, at the house of another sister.

That sister, incidentally, did the same as you: she took over the management of her family – firmly, implacably.

Her husband, who was much older than she was and had a long white beard like the saints in stained-glass windows, made wicker baskets for fishermen in a dark little room on the court.

Your sister sat enthroned behind the counter in the grocery store, where liquor was also served.

I never knew where that uncle, who made me think of the Bible, came from, and I never saw him sitting in the kitchen, much less in the drawing room, where my girl cousins played the piano.

He had his little corner, very much like a chained dog, in that room where the sun never penetrated.

You followed your bent, like the rest of them. I don't really hold it against my grandmother Simenon any more that she eyed you suspiciously when you first entered the family.

You came of another breed. And besides, you were afraid. You began to be afraid almost on the day you were born.

And with that vague, almost indefinable smile of yours, you decided to fight.

★

Every life is marked by companionships, some of long, some of brief duration. It's only at the final accounting that we can sum up and appraise the effect they have had on our destinies.

Your father died when you were five; your mother, to the best of my reckoning, when you were thirteen or fourteen.

A little later, when you went to work at the Innovation, your next companion made her appearance – Valérie, who, I'd be willing to swear, played a larger part in your life than one would think at first sight. At the age when girls exchange whispered secrets and plans for the future, Valérie, as I've said, was not pretty; in fact, she was downright ugly, for all her goodness. Are you sure it wasn't Valérie who pointed out Désiré, the man with the lovely walk, to you through the plate-glass window? Are you sure she didn't keep her eye peeled for him, just to give you pleasure?

I saw a good deal of Valérie up to the time when I left Liége at the age of nineteen. I don't believe she had changed much. Maybe she had aged just a little.

She came to dinner once a week, at first with her mother, then alone. I remember the way she looked at my father, and her titillated laughter when he teased her. And he often teased her, possibly because he liked her way of laughing.

That reminds me of a remark of yours. For some mysterious reason, maybe because Valérie's mother was very sick, you once spent the night with her. When you came home the next day, you said to me: 'I can't sleep beside a woman. A woman's smell turns my stomach.'

Those are trifling sidelights. But if I'm to reconstitute a life that's been going on for more than ninety-one years, if I'm to read in those *eyes that are looking at me and those drawn lips that tell me nothing, don't I have to search my memory for these little sidelights?*

You had a good many roomers. Three or four at a time. Some stayed only a short while, that is, they spent a year at Liège University. Others lived with us for three or four years.

You treated them all with the same patience, the same good humour, especially the poorest among them. You sat up late darning their socks.

One was so poor he had no socks at all. He lived on an egg a day and a crust of bread. You tried, with subtle ruses, to make him accept a piece of sausage or a bite of whatever we were having to eat that day. But you'd come up against a poor man who was even prouder than the poor woman you were trying to be.

I don't know what became of him. He probably became an engineer in Poland. Unless he went somewhere else to work, as I hope for his sake, because he was a Jew and he'd have died in the gas chambers.

We spent three or four Sunday afternoons with the aunt whose children you had helped to raise, the wholesale grocer's wife, who was to die of alcoholism. What went wrong between you? Or more likely between them and Désiré, because I had the impression it was because of Désiré that we stopped seeing them.

So we'd spend our Sundays with one aunt for a certain time, and then with another. But always with the aunts on your side of the family. As far as you were concerned, it was almost as if the Simenon family on the rue Puits-en-Stock didn't exist.

Every morning my father went to see his people on the way to his office, even after his mother's death. On Sunday morning all the boys and girls would be there in the kitchen, fragrant with the smell of the pot simmering on the stove. My great-grandfather, who was blind, would be sitting in his armchair, and the great-grandchildren would go over and kiss him.

My grandfather gave each of the others five centimes, and to me he gave ten. That seems odd. It wasn't that he loved me more than the others. The reason, typical of the Simenon mentality, was that I was the eldest son of his eldest son, in other words, the future head of the family.

All these images crowd in on me, Mother, as I try to understand you before you go away for good. In a day or two, or perhaps three, you will be no more. These people, motionless in their chairs in your little room, won't have anything but their own affairs to keep them busy. And I too will go back to my home and my own children.

Will they wonder about me someday as I'm wondering about you? I doubt it. In any case, I won't know.

When I left Liège, my father had just died, and it was a woman once again in mourning, in long black veils, that I left behind me. Though I was very young and without a steady job, I felt responsible and sent you a little money every month.

I wrote to you too. I don't know whether I've recovered all those letters, but I have reason to believe that they were stilted, without much feeling, for there had never been any real intimacy between us.

One scene that I've never been able to forget affected my whole adolescence. I must have been twelve or thirteen. I don't remember why, but you were very angry at me, and I stood up to you. I have to admit,

*you see, that I too was stubborn. I never gave in when I thought
I was right.*

Be that as it may, you had one of your hysterical fits, like those you
had before our Sunday outings. You lost all self-control and leaped at
me. I couldn't understand what you said, because instinctively you
spoke Flemish or German at such times. Screaming, you threw me on
the floor and began to kick me.

I finally escaped. I fled through the streets to my father's office. I
hesitated to tell him the truth. I was still trembling with pent-up fear.

'What's the matter, son?'

My father never called me Georges, but always son, as I usually call
my own sons.

I didn't tell him the whole truth. I told him you'd been angry, that
you'd lost your temper and hit me.

My father never hit me and he never hit my brother.

It's not resentment that makes me recall that scene. I bring it up
because it helps to explain your personality. For years I lived in fear
that a cab would come and take you away like your sister. There was
something excessive in your nature, something you couldn't control,
but at the same time you were very lucid.

Now I'm going to remind you of another incident, a recent one. It's
very different, and yet there's a connection.

Three or four years ago I invited you to spend some time with me
in Epalinges. Since you were very old and had never travelled by plane,
I sent my secretary to Liège to accompany you.

We fixed up the children's television room for you. One piece of
furniture we put in was a rather flimsy clothes cupboard. You ate in

your room, because you were tired and didn't feel like joining us in the dining room on the ground floor. After lunch you'd take a nap.

One day you didn't wake up at the usual hour, or even half an hour later. In the end Yole, who was then our maid, opened the door quietly. She found you sitting in a chair with black-and-blue marks on your face. You tried to put on a smile, but you were obviously in pain.

Taking advantage of our absence, you had gone over to the cupboard. Since you were too small to reach the top shelf, you had climbed up on the baseboard, and the cupboard had fallen on top of you.

Instead of calling, instead of crying out, you had crawled over to the chair and hoisted yourself up, God knows how. There you had waited stoically, your frail hands clutching the treasure you had climbed up for.

A treasure it was indeed. Little bags of gold pieces, each bag with the name of one of my children on it.

After working all your life to provide for your old age, as you put it, you had brought us the fruits of your scrimping, in gold. I still haven't given my children those bags. I'm going to wait until they've come of age, until they're settled in life, so they won't foolishly squander what it cost you so much hardship to accumulate.

The same day, you did something else, which hurt me but at the same time called forth my admiration. You came to my office and handed me an envelope containing all the money I'd sent you month after month for almost fifty years.

You wanted to be poor, you wanted to make sure of ending your life in dignity, but you didn't want to be beholden to anyone for anything, not even, perhaps especially not, to your son.

I made a mistake just now, but that's because I wasn't present when

Yole opened the door. Your face wasn't covered with black-and-blue marks, but with blood. For fear of upsetting me, they wouldn't let me see you until they'd washed the blood off. Then we called in a doctor friend of mine. I had to take you to Lausanne in an ambulance for treatment. They X-rayed you, because your ribs and one of your legs were giving you a good deal of pain.

Luckily there were no broken bones, but for several days you limped about, holding one of us by the arm.

Another detail has just come back to me. I've told you how I was haunted by the thought that a cab might stop at the door to take you where another cab had taken your sister.

Intentionally or not, you fed this fear of mine. Sometimes when you were angry, you'd suddenly cry out: 'Oh, my insides! . . . You'll see, Georges, one day you'll send me to the hospital . . .'

I was a child. I served at the six o'clock Mass in this same hospital where we are now. But at that time hospitals were mostly for paupers, and I can still see them in their striped uniforms and shaggy wool bathrobes.

The thought of your going to the hospital, of seeing you in that costume, put me into such a state that even when I was right or thought I was right, I fell down on my knees and begged your forgiveness.

And now, after all these years, both of us grown old, here we are face to face in this hospital, surrounded by wax figures.

There are two or three billion people on earth. The figure, I'm sure, is inexact, because I'm allergic to statistics and to figures in general.

How many have there been since prehistoric times? No one has any idea. What does seem reasonable to suppose is that they've always fought and killed each other as they do now, that they've always had to fight their neighbours, natural disasters, and epidemics.

But all men have asked themselves more or less the same question: 'What is man? Who is my neighbour?'

Today, ethnologists seek out the traces of these men of bygone times, who after all are our ancestors; and biologists, in laboratories all over the world, look for knowledge of present-day man.

Yet we don't know the people who live next door to us, who pass us every day in the street, who work side by side with us.

Here we are, Mother, two people looking at each other. You brought me into the world, I came out of your womb, you gave me my first milk, and yet I don't know you any more than you know me.

Here in your hospital room we're like two strangers who don't speak the same language – actually, we hardly speak at all – and who distrust each other.

And yet, believe me, it's to correct the wrong ideas I may have formed about you, to penetrate the truth of your being and learn to love you that I'm observing you, putting fragmentary memories together, and thinking.

You had your day of triumph, though I can't date it, not even approximately.

When I was twenty, you were about forty, and it struck me as almost indecent that you could still make love. As I saw it, your time was up, you were beginning to be an old woman.

I'm not the only one to have felt that way. I can read the same astonishment in the eyes of my son and daughter. I'm sure it's the same in the house next door and any other house.

To me you were a widow. You had lived out your life. No further changes were to be expected.

And yet a change did come, and a very important one, because it finally made the dreams of your youth and adult years come true.

I don't remember where I was when I got the news. Was I in France, in Africa, or in the United States? In any case, I received a letter in your nervous, angular hand, telling me that you were remarrying.

I have to admit that at the time I was shocked. I still worshipped my father so that the thought of you replacing him seemed inconceivable. I understood when I read the details. You had just married a retired train conductor, a conductor on the North Belgian Railway, where Monsieur Reculé had also been employed.

At last you had a pension coming to you. At last, your old age, come what might, was provided for.

Later on, I received photographs and postcards. You, who had scarcely set foot out of Outremeuse, went to Lourdes, Nice, Ostende, and heaven knows where else. And you travelled free of charge, because your new husband was entitled to a certain number of kilometres each year that didn't cost him a penny.

You sent me his picture too. He was a lean, wiry Ardennais, with hard-cut features and a rather inexpressive look.

I met him only once, on one of my visits to Liège. At that time, the household was still fairly peaceful. Neither of you ever told me where you'd met. But you did tell me you had cared for his sick wife up to her last breath.

He wasn't from our neighbourhood. He had lived at the opposite end of town.

I wondered, just as I had in connection with Désiré:

Where? How?

But you don't ask your mother such questions.

'*How is Valérie getting along?*'

She'd gone a long way with you and you had exchanged so many intimate thoughts. You answered drily: '*I don't see her any more.*'

And then you added with a bit of a forced smile: '*Can you imagine? She's jealous because I've remarried.*'

Strangely enough, though you'd replaced my father with another man, you kept his name. Your new husband's last name was André. Yet in your letters and even in certain official papers that came my way, you wrote: *Madame André Simenon.*

That hurt me. It seemed a breach of trust. Another man had taken my father's place in your house and bed, but you were determined to keep your first husband's name.

Was it because I was already famous? Was the name a kind of talisman to you?

I thought so. I even thought that in your heart of hearts you too continued to worship big Désiré, and that even after remarrying you wanted to keep this tie with him.

In your hospital room I've been forced to change my mind.

Don't imagine, Mother, that I hold it against you or that I judge you. I judge no one. If men have been killing each other since prehistoric times, isn't it because they've failed to understand their neighbours, the members of the neighbouring tribe?

You became Madame André, the wife of a civil servant, entitled to a pension for himself and after his death for his wife. Nevertheless, you insisted on remaining Madame Simenon.

I saw the man you called Père André only once. He didn't strike me as unpleasant or eccentric or neurotic.

All I remember his telling me was that being a train conductor was one of the hardest and most exacting jobs in the world, that the constant vibrations were a permanent danger to one's health, and that his greatest pleasure in life was doing a bit of gardening every day around a tiny little house that he owned on the hill. That was the little house where he'd lived for twenty years with his first wife, the woman you had taken such good care of during her last illness, Mother.

When I look at you now and think of that part of your past, I'm rather surprised at your serenity.

You and Père André soon began to distrust each other. He accused you of being impatient for him to die, so you'd have the pension all to yourself. God only knows whether he also accused you of hastening the death of his first wife.

There were no more roomers on the rue de l'Enseignement. The two of you were alone, face to face, two strangers if not enemies. No one recorded the words you exchanged. They must have been terrible, full of deep-seated hatred, for one day you decided to stop talking to each other and to exchange scribbled notes when communication was necessary.

When I speak of hatred, I'm not exaggerating. True, I wasn't there. But when a husband and wife living under the same roof get to the point where each does his own cooking, each keeping his provisions in his own locked food cupboard, and one waits for the other to vacate the kitchen before getting his own dinner, what other explanation is there?

43

You were both afraid of being poisoned. It had become an obsession with you, perhaps a kind of madness.

I can't help thinking of your sister and the cab that took her away while a man braced his arms against the wall and sobbed.

And yet you lived like that for several years. You did your shopping. And he did his. You cooked your meal. He waited till you'd finished eating and then he cooked his.

And the rest of the time? You couldn't spend the whole day sitting silently together in the kitchen or living room. He went out to his little garden on the hill, and you no doubt dropped in on a neighbour for a cup of coffee. There's no denying it, you had won. You'd won the pension you'd dreamed of all your life. You weren't ashamed of that money, because one day you came to me and proudly returned all the money I had sent you.

Père André died. Suddenly he collapsed, just as my father had done.

I wish I knew what you were thinking at this moment, what images were running through your mind. Sometimes you seem to be dozing blissfully, and sometimes there's an almost mocking smile on your face.

Whom are you mocking? Désiré? Père André? Me and all the others sitting motionless in your room? The nun impassively telling her beads?

Maybe it's life you're mocking, because you probably see it in a different light when you're about to lose it.

*

As soon as the sun begins to shine on this enormous courtyard in the midst of the hospital buildings, patients in uniform make their appearance on the benches. I too have got into the habit of appearing at about ten o'clock. Before that the nurses are busy with you, and your room has to be swept and put in order.

Sometimes at this time of day no one is here but the nun. I make it sound as if it is always the same nun. That's unlikely, but because of their habit, their immobility and their pallor, I can't tell them apart.

'How are you, Georges?'

You smile at me.

Have you been waiting for me? Does my twice-daily visit give you pleasure? Would you rather be left alone with the distant relatives, neighbours, and strangers who will soon start filing in? I don't know. In any case, you've never felt the need to say anything to me, to give me some personal message.

Yesterday I went with Teresa to visit the chapel where I so often served at Mass. I was curious to know whether my memories were deceiving me, whether it was really beautiful. It was built several centuries ago by a certain Ernest of Bavaria. Who was he? A count, a duke, a prince, an emperor? It doesn't matter much. We've had so many foreign rulers in Liège.

What gives the chapel a special cachet is that it was built on two levels. The patients gather on the ground floor. Ten or twelve steps lead to the upper level. That's where the high altar is, facing the congregation, and on each side there's a gallery reserved for the nuns.

On Sunday there were two Masses, one at six o'clock as on other days, and another, more solemn one, at eight. Between the two I was taken to a dining room, where I was given two soft-boiled eggs, bread and butter, and coffee.

What I remember most vividly is the smell. Not only the flat smell of the room, which is known to me from other convents, but also the smell and even the taste of the bread and butter, the eggs, and the coffee.

I asked a nun who was passing by whether the former vestry nun was still alive. Someone went to get her. She is now an old woman, who doesn't hear very well, see very well, or, I had the impression, understand very well.

Of course she didn't recognize me. I wanted to check up on a memory. On Sundays and holidays I wore a fine lace surplice. Someone would unfold it with great care and put it over me with slow, gingerly movements.

Had that been only in my imagination? I finally made myself understood by the nun, the very same sister who had taken care of these surplices and dressed me in them. She opened some drawers. She took out the little wooden boxes in which these precious vestments were packed.

I spoke to her of the days when I had served at Mass, when I had put this surplice on, but my words awakened no memory in her.

Some days I crossed the courtyard a few steps ahead of the padre. In one hand I held a long, black wooden pole with a silver cross at the end of it. In the other I held a bell; all the patients we passed knew what that meant.

We were on our way to give extreme unction to one of their number, who was a few steps ahead of them. In the ward there were at least twenty beds, and these patients also understood. They propped themselves up on one elbow and crossed themselves.

Those were the moments I liked least. They got me down.

*Yet death in itself didn't upset me. Two or three times a week there
would be a Mass for the dead. And though I was paid only two francs
a month for the daily morning Masses, I received fifty centimes for
each requiem Mass, because funeral expenses were taken care of by
the city. And on some mornings there would be two Masses for the
dead, one right after the other.*

*Teresa and I took our lunches in town. We never went to a big res-
taurant. We went to so-called fry shops, and as I've told you, our menu
was almost always the same: mussels, French fried potatoes and occa-
sionally eel.*

*During the two or three weeks you spent with us in Epalinges after
the cupboard with the gold pieces had fallen on you, I hesitated to let
you return to Belgium. You weren't in the best of health and I didn't
like to think of you alone in your little house. And you obstinately
refused to let me hire a companion to keep an eye on you. If the word
'obstinate' applies to anyone, it's to you. For several years I tried to
have a bathroom installed in your house. You wouldn't let the plumb-
ers in. I got you to accept a television set, but it took me more than
two years.*

*It's true that once you had it you made good use of it. Hardly any
of the neighbours had television, and half the street gathered in your
house almost every evening.*

*Even so, you were too much alone to suit me. One afternoon you
fell on the pavement and couldn't get up until a policeman happened
to come along. I don't know if you were bleeding at the knees or elbows.
What I do know is that the policeman wanted to take you to the hospital. You answered in your mixture of Liège and Flemish accents.*

'Oh no, monsieur. There's nothing wrong with me. My house is

only a few steps away. Just see me home and I'll open a bottle of good wine.'

The policeman had no more luck than I. He wanted to have you examined, but you refused; you wouldn't even see a neighbourhood doctor. He simply had to go in with you and drink the wine you served him.

You see that the word 'obstinate' seems to have been made to order for you.

But what if one day you'd felt incapable of getting out of bed? If you hadn't been able to go to the rue Puits-en-Stock for groceries?

I didn't want to let you go back. I discussed it with my doctor in Epalinges, who saw you several times. He told me it would do no good to cross you, no good at all.

My idea was to move you into one of those rest homes between Geneva and Montreux, only a few miles from my place. They're nothing like old people's homes, not at all gloomy or sinister, more like luxury hotels.

But luxury is just what you didn't want. You didn't want to go to a rest home. What you wanted, wanted with all your heart, was your home, the house you'd managed to pay for after years of hard work and that was finally yours.

I'm convinced that some of the people on the rue de l'Enseignement think I'm a 'bad son', that I deserted you, possibly left you destitute.

It took a letter from one of my cousins, a woman of almost your age who went to see you now and then, to make me assert my authority and go against your will.

You hadn't left the house in several days. Some meat, a piece of cake, and so on, were rotting away in the icebox, and that's what you were living on.

Because you didn't want to give in. Do you understand? I under-stood very well. My doctor had even said: 'If you uproot her, you'll hasten her end.'

But was I to let you eat spoiled food, to risk having a worried neighbour break your door in and find that you'd been dead for a week or two?

I made inquiries. I found a lovely house in the country, not far from Liège, with an enormous garden. Some nuns lived there and took in a few boarders, who, I was able to convince myself, received the best of care.

I had a wall taken out so as to make a little living room for you. I also had a bathroom put in. It was your own apartment; you wouldn't be dependent on anyone.

I took you there. More than ever you had that slightly mocking and at the same time resigned smile on your face. You consented to stay, but you weren't happy about it. And after a few days, despite the cosy comfort, you insisted on being taken back to your little house.

'But sister, what if somebody breaks in and robs me, seeing the house is empty?'

You were almost ninety and still you worried about being robbed. Robbed of what? Your furniture? Your linen? A few souvenirs you'd brought back from your trips with your second husband – a shell from Ostende, a statuette of the Virgin?

Twice they had to take you back to the house to make sure the doors were really locked. Then one day they had to bring you to the Hôpital de Bavière for an operation.

That was another visit. I went to see you. You'd withstood the shock of the operation amazingly, and by the time I got there, you were up and about.

My friend Orban couldn't get over it.

'I never expected her to pull through. Now she's taken out a new lease on life. Another few months.'

What a glitter of triumph, of defiance in your grey-blue eyes!

★

Here's a strange thing. Ordinarily I'm very much aware of the weather, of a sunlit pavement, a dark, cloudy sky, the north wind, or the föhn. Yet during the time I spent in Liège, I hardly know if it was six days, or maybe eight or ten, all I remember is unbroken greyness, like pencil lines on white paper.

One morning when we were alone except for the inevitable nun, you asked me: 'What are you going to do with the house?'

This was the first time since I'd been with you in the room where you were slowly dying that you spoke, even indirectly, of death. When I was a child and then a young man, you often spoke of it, I'd almost say with a certain satisfaction. 'When I'm dead, children . . . ' Or: 'You'll understand when I'm gone . . . '

But that was more than fifty years ago. Now that death is lurking in your room, so to speak, you don't say a word about it. You don't seem to fear it. I imagine that you accept it and that sometimes you're even a little impatient to find it so slow in coming.

'What are you going to do with the house?'

I repeated what I'd said years before: 'I'll leave it to my nephew intact.'

'With the furniture, the linen, and everything else?'

I'd made that promise to my brother. He died at about the same age as my father, somewhere between forty and forty-five, leaving a widow and a son who was already of age. They both made a good living. But I wouldn't dream of accepting any part of my mother's estate.

During one of my rare visits to Liège, you gave me a long, inquiring look and said these words that I've never been able to forget: 'What a pity, Georges, that it's Christian who had to die.'

Did you mean that in your heart of hearts you wished I'd gone first?

And, come to think of it, you added: 'He was so tender, so affectionate . . .'

And of course I wasn't, or at least I didn't show it.

The house! The house! Really and truly yours. Bricks, windows, doors, that belonged to you and no one else. You were past eighty when my cousin Maria, your last close relative, who was about the same age as you and who still wrote to me now and then, told me she'd found you at the top of a ladder, painting the walls of the hallway. You painted the walls of the yard too.

Your house wasn't just a house: it was a symbol. It symbolized the final victory of the little girl from the rue Féronstrée, the triumph of your will.

The people who lived in the Outremeuse quarter were what for want of a better term I should call 'humble folk'. The main street is the narrow, bustling rue Puits-en-Stock. The streetcar with its perpetual ringing seems to wind its way between the shops.

That's the Outremeuse of the Simenons. You seldom set foot in the glassed-in kitchen, and you hardly knew my uncles, my aunts, and their children. I have no idea how many cousins we had on that side, as we called it. About thirty? I doubt if that's a great exaggeration. And on Sunday morning every one of them turned up for his five-centime piece.

The belfry of Saint-Nicolas was hardly a quarter of a mile away. Before flying the coop when I was nineteen and a half, I lived with it, though in two or three different houses. Like your house, all of them were in the shadow of the belfry of Saint-Nicolas.

We moved because our lease expired, or because you'd found something a little bigger. The furniture was put in the exact same places, for all the houses in the neighbourhood were built on pretty much the same plan.

The neighbourhood is inhabited by old people with small pensions, clerks, foremen, widows, in other words humble folk, and I still regard myself as one of them.

Your house was the last, a few steps from the one I lived in before I went away to Paris. I've never slept there. I never stayed more than an hour or two, on my way through.

The last few times I went to see you, I was bewildered. I'd always known the same dining-room furniture, more or less in Henri II style, with carved lions' heads at the four corners of the table, the buffet with its multicoloured glass, the chairs with their imitation cordovan seats.

One fine day I discovered two dining-room sets that were almost alike, two buffets with coloured glass, and some armchairs I had never seen before.

The strangest, I hesitate to say the most amusing, part of it was that you yourself didn't know what was what. You see, you had in *your house the furniture you and my father bought when you were married long ago; but you also had Père André's furniture, which was almost the same. And you yourself made mistakes. You said to me, for instance: 'Look, Georges, that's the table you wrote Au Pont des Arches on.'*

It wasn't that table at all. It was another, which I'd never seen, which had been used in a household of which I knew nothing.

And you've never been able to tell me what became of that other table of highly polished mahogany, with just the kind of sheen that I love. You swore it was the one you pointed out, but even then I knew you'd given it to Cousin Maria, your last close relative.

Because, being the little last-born, much younger than your brothers and sisters, you were the only living member of your immediate family; the other survivor wasn't a sister but a niece, who, give or take a year or so, was the same age as you and in about as bad shape.

After the state of her health prevented her from visiting you, I had little news of you except for your letters, which were few and far between. But you were getting muddled – you mixed up your dates and even the phases of your life, so much so that you sometimes spoke of Père André as your father.

Now in your hospital bed are you still getting people and dates mixed up? I doubt it. The look on your face is amazingly lucid. True, you don't talk much, especially when you're surrounded by visitors, as you almost always are.

But that doesn't prevent you from wanting what you want.

'Listen, Georges. You know I've never liked the tombstone you put up for your father . . .'

A large slab of unpolished granite with nothing on it but a name and a date. I've always detested mortuary monuments, statutes, columns, portraits embedded in the stone.

'They say it's beginning to settle . . .'

It's not indifference on my part, far from it. I worshipped big Désiré and still do. But I've never given much thought to his grave. I've never gone there to meditate. When I need to feel him near me, my thoughts are enough.

This time, Mother, without suspecting the enormity of what you were saying, you added: 'I'd rather be buried in the vault with Père André and his wife.'

I was dumbfounded. After so many years you'd ended up by confusing the two men with whom you had shared parts of your life. Did you really love my father? Today I wonder. The plans you made from the start of your marriage were not for the two of you, but just for yourself.

You were already thinking of the house, and you put money aside without telling him. True, it was your money. It was the money you made by looking after your roomers. Even so, it was a kind of private nest egg, if I may say so, and to my mind that implies the exact opposite of love.

It's true that you didn't love Père André any more than you did my father. I wonder, incidentally, why you called him Père André. He wasn't anybody's father. He never had any children. And he never had anything to do with the priesthood.

Yet he was Père André. My father was Désiré.

The house on the rue de la Loi had two rooms on the ground floor, not counting the kitchen with the glass door at the end of the hallway. Those two rooms were both cluttered with dining-room furniture and old armchairs. The walls were covered with photographs of Christian, of me, of Père André and his wife, and of his father.

In other words, two families were mixed on the walls, and there were two sets of furniture that you yourself couldn't tell apart. You attributed to a young couple what had actually belonged to a retired train conductor.

I've been married twice. I'm living with a third woman. But it would never occur to me to mix my memories.

My children know the origin of every piece of furniture, every picture, every knickknack.

But I'm pretty sure they're not interested.

You see, Mother, I have nothing to reproach you with, and I don't reproach you. You had your aim in life and you pursued it with rare perseverance.

You succeeded. Maybe that is why, as you lie in your hospital bed, your look is so serene, and why there's sometimes a spark of irony in your eyes.

If I wanted to be vulgar, I'd say: 'You've got one over the lot of them!'

*

My dear Mama, you see that I've gone back to the same words, or almost, as in the beginning of my letter, probably because I'm just as moved now as I was then.

One night, when I'd just undressed and was about to go to bed, the hospital called to tell me you were dead. I'd been expecting it from one minute to the next. The reality came as a violent shock all the same.

I threw on my clothes and rushed to the hospital, to your little room that I had grown accustomed to, forgetting that my visits there were bound to end.

I found your face serene, with a serenity that does not exist in life.

I kissed you on the forehead as I had kissed my father, and I sat down beside you. The nun was still there, as motionless as if nothing had happened. I asked her if you had suffered, and she said no.

In spite of myself, I went on thinking. The week we had just spent together, hardly speaking to one another, left me with a sense of loss. It seemed to me that our week wasn't complete, that we hadn't fully made contact.

And I didn't want to let you go without coming to know you and understand you. Your eyes, now, were expressionless, but had an unearthly fixity. Your lips, once and for all, were set in a mysterious line that I couldn't interpret. Irony, appeasement, or something else? I'm inclined to say appeasement.

They had laid you out. You were beautiful. You were regal, imperial on your little bed, and we who had gathered around you were mere mortals, with all our hesitations, petty problems and anxieties.

I went on thinking. I went on trying to understand you. And I realized that all your life you had been good.

Not necessarily in the eyes of others, but in your own, and in your secret heart. You had struggled to reach the goal that the little five-year-old girl had set herself. You had gritted your teeth. But you needed, you always needed, to feel that you were good. And that,

Mother, is why you sacrified yourself all your life. You sacrificed your-self for every unfortunate who came your way, whether married and in difficulties or single and lonely; I almost said for everyone who passed in the street.

For everyone there were treasures of tenderness and patience in your heart. Nothing discouraged you. On the contrary, the harder the problem, the more you threw yourself into it.

Is it surprising that you didn't take much interest in people you regarded as the spoiled darlings of fortune?

That was us. You had no eyes for us, or you classified us as 'the ones who have everything'.

You came from the bottom – one of those who had received nothing as a gift, for whom every little pleasure was a conquest, something to be won by struggle.

You went on fighting. Your job wasn't finished. You had worked with your roomers until we went to high school. As you saw it, our future was provided for.

But not yours, nor that of the other people you met when you went shopping in the neighbourhood.

Your feeling for us wasn't goodness, it was mother love.

But you had to be good. Not only in the eyes of others. You expected no thanks or gratitude. You absolutely had to feel that you were good.

And after the week I spent at your deathbed, I believe that I finally discovered the truth.

Like your father, like most of your brothers and sisters, you were born with a certain morbid tendency, today we'd call it neurosis. All of you were hyperly sensitive, highly strung. Some of you tried in vain to get by with drink.

The little last-born, who had seen the whole family engaged in this struggle, and seen some of its members gradually falling to pieces, decided when she was very young to save herself by her own resources.

That was the little girl with the hazy, almost white hair at the Innovation. That was Valérie's friend. That was the girl who admired Désiré's lovely walk and later his lovely way of lifting his hat.

Once married, with a mewling child, you realized that this wasn't enough. You rented a house. You took in roomers. You subjected yourself to the life of a slave.

Up to the time of Désiré's death. How many years later did you remarry? I don't know. You got what you'd been aiming at: security, your famous pension.

How can I hold it against you? I know that during the war you hid gold pieces in a pile of coal. People might have thought it was avarice and that you were saving them for yourself. But at the same time you were crocheting little bags for all my children.

I sent you plenty of money to live on. One day you came to me and returned it all.

You see, Mother, you're one of the most complicated people I've ever known. Often, in thinking of you, I've remembered the cab that came to take your sister away. What stood between you and me was the merest nothing.

That nothing was your ferocious need to be good, in the eyes of others, but most of all perhaps in your own.